To Barbara
With Love
Cliff and Diane
Christmas
1999

CATS
IN ART

Janice Anderson

A Compilation of Works from the
BRIDGEMAN ART LIBRARY

SMITHMARK

Cats in Art

This edition published in 1996 by SMITHMARK
Publishers, a division of U.S. Media Holdings, Inc.,
16 East 32nd Street, New York, NY 10016.
SMITHMARK books are available for bulk
purchase for sales promotion and premium use.
For details write or call the manager of special
sales, SMITHMARK Publishers, 16 East 32nd
Street, New York, NY 10016; (212) 532-6600
First published in Great Britain in 1996 by
Parragon Books Limited
Units 13-17, Avonbridge Industrial Estate
Atlantic Road, Avonmouth, Bristol BS11 9QD
United Kingdom

© Parragon Books Limited 1996

ISBN 0-7651-9892-4

Printed in Italy

Editors:	Barbara Horn, Alexa Stace, Alison Stace, Tucker Slingsby Ltd and Jennifer Warner
Designers:	Robert Mathias • Pedro Prá-Lopez, Kingfisher Design Services
Typesetting/DTP:	Frances Prá-Lopez, Kingfisher Design Services
Picture Research:	Kathy Lockley

The publishers would like to thank Joanna Hartleyat the Bridgeman Art Library
for her invaluable help.

CATS IN ART

Cats are an immensely popular subject today, both with artists and art lovers. Three of the most popular postcards on sale at London's Tate Gallery are of cat pictures, including two in this book, William Hogarth's The Graham Children and David Hockney's *Mr and Mrs Clark and Percy* (page 74).

Although cats have had a recognized place in the art of the Far East for centuries, from early prints, woodcuts and sculpture to more recent paintings, especially watercolours, this has not always been true of Western art. The Ancient Eygptians included cats in wall-paintings and on at least one papyrus, and of course there were many carvings and sculptures of the Eygptian cat gods. There is also a rare Greek depiction of a cat on a 5th-century BC statue, and the Romans included cats in mosaics.

For centuries after the Romans, however, the cat's place in Western art, if it appeared at all, was, as in life, in the home and in the background. Whether discreetly incorporated in an illumination in the Irish Book of Kells, a very early representation of a cat in Western art, or set down amidst the busy orderliness of a 17th century Dutch kitchen, the cat was seen as unimportant and everyday. Cats were not felt to add any particular cachet to a painting, especially if it were a portrait. Great men and women were often painted surrounded by dogs and horses, children and possessions, but seldom with their cats.

In late medieval times, in northern Europe in particular, the cat suffered dreadful persecution as a result of religious superstition. It was an attitude reflected in art, where the cat was most often to be found in woodcuts depicting witches' sabbaths in sensational detail, with witches flying about on broomsticks, accompanied by black cats.

Yet, even while fanatics in northern Europe were torturing cats in the name of religion, cats in Italy, if we can judge by the art of the time, were seen as part of everyday domestic life. Antonello da Messina included a small cat sitting companionably near the saint in *St Jerome in His Study* (page 8), Paolo Veronese showed cats at the feet of Christ in more than one painting, while Leonardo da Vinci's drawings of cats, apparently done while they played at his feet, are well known.

Throughout European art in the 17th century, the cat was still appearing, on the whole, in a domestic role. Many of the interiors painted by Dutch artists included cats, and in France artists such as Louis le Nain would put neatly relaxed little cats in their peasant genre paintings. There were exceptions, such as a couple of Tintoretto paintings of religious subjects – an Annunciation and a Last Supper – in both of which the cats look distinctly malevolent, as if Tintoretto saw them as symbols of wickedness and devilry.

In some ways, things got worse for the cat in art in the 18th century. While its domestic role was extended by its inclusion in the still lifes of such master painters as Chardin and Desportes, this was also the time when the cat began turning up in pictures as the plaything of courtesans and prostitutes. In contrast, however, the cat was also being seen as a suitable companion for young girls, with artists such as Peronneau using the cat as a symbol of innocence in many charming pastel portraits.

It was during the latter half of the 19th century that the cat in Western society was brought out of the kitchen and into the drawing-room, as it were, a change reflected in art. Manet included a cat in a portrait of his wife, while Renoir did numerous paintings of charming girls and young women with equally charming cats.

By the beginning of the 20th century, the cat was even being considered as a pleasantly relaxed companion for men in portraits. Hitherto, with a few exceptions like the portrait of the great 16th century Genoese admiral, Andrea Doria, which included two of his cats, and one of Sir Walter Scott which showed his cat, Hinx, spread out on his desk, the cat had been seen as rather too effeminate a companion to be included in serious male portraiture. Now, the cat began turning up on the knees of artists, critics and men of letters; Pierre Bonnard included a cat in his portrait of the art dealer and publisher Ambroise Vollard, Edouard Vuillard in his portrait of the eminent critic Théodore Vuillard, and Henry Tonks in his delightful study of Philip Wilson Steer and Walter Sickert (page 71).

At the same time, artists began looking at the cat as a suitable, even inspiring, subject for study in its own right. Back in the 18th century, the great English animal painter, George Stubbs, had done only one true portrait of a domestic cat in all his tremendous output. Now, cats seemed to be everywhere. Pierre Bonnard, with his superb White Cat of 1894, was one of the first off the mark with a cat study. After him came the exceptionally fine watercolours of Gwen John and the vividly brilliant oil paintings of Franz Marc. Pablo Picasso, at the outbreak of the Second World War, painted a fierce cat with a desperately fluttering bird between its teeth: the cat was as suitable a vehicle for expressing his feelings about world events as were the horse and bull in his painting, Guernica.

Although there is a tendency for 'cat art' to become overworked, falling into the same sentimental trap which bedevilled so much late-Victorian animal art, on the whole the cat's place in art today is assured. It is a relaxed place, often centred on the private life and home of the artist and his friends, as in the watercolours of Edward Bawden or in David Hockney's painting mentioned earlier. In the best art, it is also a place where the cat remains itself.

Detail

▷ **St Jerome in His Study**
Antonello da Messina (d 1479)

Wood panel

THE 4TH-CENTURY SAINT, Jerome, who was born in Dalmatia, was one of the most learned of the early fathers of the church and a famed biblical scholar. He spent two years doing penance in the desert, where his only companions were wild animals. One of the best-known stories about St Jerome tells how he tamed a lion by pulling a thorn out of its paw, and depictions of the saint in art show him accompanied by a lion. Antonello da Messina, an artist from the south of Italy about whose life and early career little is known, has followed tradition by including a lion holding up its right paw in his picture of St Jerome. But he has also added a surprisingly domestic touch in the form of a small grey cat which sits, its front paws tucked under its chest, not far from the saint's feet.

◁ **Garden of Earthly Delights:
Adam and Eve in the
Garden of Eden** c1500
Hieronymus Bosch
(c1450–1516)

Oil on panel

ALTHOUGH HIERONYMUS BOSCH,
the Dutch-born master of the
fantastical in art, has included
a cat in the left wing of his
triptych, The Garden of
Earthly Delights, it is not a
jolly, sit-by-the-hearth kind of
cat he has chosen to depict.
This cat is a hunter, his latest
kill dangling from his jaws as
he stalks past Adam. It is as
though Bosch has chosen the
cat a symbol of the kind
of experiences Adam and Eve
will encounter when their
innocence is lost and they are
forced out of the Garden of
Eden. Even in the Garden
of Eden, Bosch saw evil
and portrayed it in the shape
of a cat.

▷ **The Entrance of the Animals into the Ark**
Jacopo da Ponte Bassano
(c 1510–92)

Oil

JACOPO DA PONTE was the best of a family of Venetian painters who took the name Bassano after the small town in which they lived and worked in the 16th and 17th centuries. While Jacopo has managed to get several stocky human figures into this lively painting, his main effort is concentrated on the extraordinary collection of animals, both wild and domestic, which fill the canvas. He has included both kinds of cat. Wild cats are represented by the pair of lions marching up the gangplank towards the wonderfully un-ship-like Ark, both of them looking more like statues of the Venetian Lion of St Mark than the real thing. The domestic cats, on the other hand, appear to have been observed in real life. They crouch, one a dark tabby and the other black and white, in a very lifelike manner among the birds and animals in the foreground.

Feast in the House of the Levi 1573
Paolo Veronese (1528–88)

Fresco

◁ *Previous pages 12-13*

THIS ENORMOUS, CROWDED
scene, full of light and colour
and set against a Palladian-style
architectural background, is
typical of the work of Paolo
Veronese, who was born in
Verona and did his greatest
work in Venice. Despite their
religious themes, his paintings
are redolent of the gorgeous,
licencious magnificence of
16th century Venice – a style
which was to get him into
trouble with the Inquisition,
who saw a great deal of profanity
in what were supposed to be
religious works. This famous
painting, one of the glories of
the Accademia in Venice, is
believed to have been planned
by Vernonese as a Last Supper,
but was re-named when its
style and contents were
criticized. The playful cat at
Christ's feet, which the large
dog may be eyeing with
thoughts of attack in mind, was
probably one of the 'scurrilities'
to which the Inquisitor objected
when questioning Veronese
about the contents of his
religious pictures.

▷ **Interior with a Woman
Knitting, a Serving Woman
and a Child** c 1660
Pieter de Hooch (1629–c 84)

Oil on canvas

THIS PAINTING IS TYPICAL of the
work of the Dutch genre artist,
Pieter de Hooch, whose finest
domestic interiors, notable for
the quality of the light playing
over their surfaces, were
painted over a decade or so
while he was living in Delft. His
subjects varied little: usually
two or three people engaged
in domestic tasks in an interior
room, with light coming in
through an open door allowing
a glimpse of another room and,
sometimes, the outside world.
In this picture, the finely dressed
lady – presumably the mistress
of the house – is knitting while
the child offers her a dish.
The cat sitting by the lady's
footstool looks well-fed and
part of the family: he is
not there just to catch mice.

◁ **Merrymaking in a Tavern** c 1670–74

Jan Havicksz Steen (1626–79)

Oil on canvas

JAN STEEN WAS BORN in Leiden and after studying with several leading Dutch painters of the day settled in Haarlem, where he built up a reputation as a painter of lively genre scenes. He moved back to Leiden in the last decade of his life, keeping an inn there for some time. To judge by this picture, Steen's inn was a pleasantly relaxed sort of place, where everyone felt free to enjoy themselves, without getting unpleasantly drunk. The cat happily eating the boy's left-over food, untroubled by the dog sniffing at him, adds an attractive domestic touch in the foreground.

◁ **The Ray** 1728
Jean-Baptiste Siméon Chardin
(1699–1779)

Oil on canvas

FRENCH 18TH CENTURY it may
be, but this still life, which is
very much a picture of kitchen
life, harks back to Dutch
interior paintings of the 17th
century. It is an early work by
Chardin, one of France's finest
still-life 18th century painters,
and was painted in the year he
became a member of the
French Academy. The cat
seems to have been included
in this picture, as in Dutch
interiors, to emphasize its
domestic nature: cats did not
yet have a recognized place in
European drawing-rooms. Like
every other object in the
painting, the little cat is
wonderfully well observed,
painted with great delicacy
yet with considerable depth
of tone.

△ **The Distressed Poet** c 1735 William Hogarth (1697–1764)

Oil on canvas

WILLIAM HOGARTH BEGAN painting 'modern moral subjects' early in the 1730s, partly for economic reasons: portrait painting had become a kind of drudgery and not 'sufficiently paid to provide what my family required'. But he was also concerned to depict and comment upon the morality and mores of his time. In this lively painting Hogarth depicts a poet working on a manuscript instead of paying the milkmaid, who has erupted into the room loudly presenting her account board; he is also failing to note that the dog is making off with the family's dinner joint, left on a chair beneath an ominously bare cupboard. The one quiet point in the chaos is the cat, quietly feeding her two kittens – making a bed for them on the poet's coat, tossed on the floor.

Detail

◁ **The Graham Children** 1742
William Hogarth (1697–1764)

Oil on canvas

THE FOUR HANDSOME CHILDREN
in this superb portrait were
the family of Daniel Graham,
who was apothecary to Chelsea
Hospital in London. Not
content with producing a
simple family group, Hogarth
seems to have introduced a
note of allegory into the picture.
The figure of Cupid on top
of the clock on the left of the
picture holds a scythe, suggesting
the passing of time, while
Orpheus and his lute still make
music, if only as a carving on
the side of the boy's toy organ
box. But we are still in the
innocent world of childhood:
the splendid tabby cat, his
claws at the ready and his
great golden eyes glowing with
anticipation, will not kill the
bird, for it is safe in its
ornate cage.

◁ **Young Girl with a Cat** 1747
Jean-Baptiste Perroneau
(1715–83)

Pastel

ONE OF THE GLORIES of the
Louvre's superb collection of
pastels, this exceptionally fine
drawing shows Perroneau
adding a gamut of green and
blue shadings into the
traditional rose pinks and
blues of 18th century French
pastels. Where contempories
like Boucher and Lépicié
included cats as subtle erotic
symbols in paintings of women
at their toilette, Perroneau
here depicts the cat as a wholly
suitable companion for an
innocent young girl. It was a
theme he was to repeat,
notably in a pastel in the
National Gallery in London,
Girl with a Kitten.

△ **Miss Ann White's Kitten** George Stubbs (1724–1806)

Oil on canvas

FAMOUS FOR HIS brilliant studies of horses and dogs, and for big cats, including lions, tigers, cheetahs and leopards, George Stubbs ventured into portraying a domestic cat in detail only once, with this charming kitten. It is possible that he did not feel as easy with small cats as with other animals because their thick fur disguised their anatomy, reducing the value of the enormously detailed anatomical studies which Stubbs had made a essential part of his artistic training. Despite this, Miss Ann White's kitten is a very realistic little animal, the typical pose and clear, still gaze well caught by the artist's brush.

◁ **Don Manuel Osorio de Zuniga** c 1786–8
Francisco Jose de Goya y
Lucientes (1746–1828)

Oil on canvas

THIS WONDERFUL PORTRAIT dates
from a particularly fertile
period in the life of the great
Spanish painter, Goya. Among
his many portraits of the period
were a number of children,
and this is one of the best known,
memorable for its clear,
uncomplicated style, free of
unnecessary detail. Goya has
turned the same clear gaze on
the little boy's pet cats and
birds: no mere decorative
elements, all three are depicted
as creatures full of life and
character. The bird holds in its
beak a card bearing a print of
a bird and the artist's signature.
The cats gaze intently,
malevolently at the bird: their
interest does not bode well.
Perhaps Goya is hinting here
at allegory, reminding us of the
inevitable end of all
innocence, whether of animal
or child.

△ **Cat with Her Kittens in a Basket** 1797 Samuel de Wilde (1748–1832)

Oil on canvas

BY THE END of the 18th century, social change and the Romantic Movement had done much to alter people's attitude to the world about them. Nature, in the ascendency among people of taste and education, had become a worthwhile subject for study in its own right. Artists treated animals as suitable subjects for portraits, though cats were still a relatively uncommon subject for such paintings: dogs and horses, lions and leopards were all considered much more noble subjects than mere cats. Samuel de Wilde's fine study of a tortoiseshell cat and her kittens is unusual for its time, and is free of the sentimentality and anthropomorphism which spoilt much 19th century animal art.

Detail

▷ **Portrait of Louise Vernet as a Child** c 1810
Théodore Géricault (1791–1824)

Oil on canvas

AMONG THE WORK of this French artist are numerous sketches, drawings and paintings of domestic cats, in which the artist concentrates on the grace of their movements or the shapes of their heads. Often, his studies of domestic cats look like small versions of big, wild cats; the remarkably solid domestic cat in this picture, sitting quietly with its young owner, is one such, for its head has more the appearance of a panther than of a domestic cat. The child, Louise Vernet, was a young relative of Carle Vernet, the painter with whom Géricault studied as a pupil from 1808 to 1810.

▷ **Chinese Cat Merchants**
1843

Engraving

THIS LIVELY SCENE, painted by
Thomas Allom (1804–72) in
the first half of the 19th
century, was published in 1843
as one of a series of engravings
called 'China in a Series of
Views' by G N Wright.
Although the cat is believed
to have first been domesticated
in Eygpt, the Chinese have
known the cat for centuries;
like the Eygptians, they once
included the cat in religious
observances, having an
agricultural god in cat form.
By the time this scene was
recorded, cats had become
of sufficient importance in the
Chinese economy, particularly
as rat-catchers, to warrant
having merchants devoted to
their sale.

△ **Sleeping Cat** c 1850

Japanese watercolour

THIS SPLENDID TABBY CAT has remained inscrutably still and asleep long enough to allow the anonymous artist to produce a superbly detailed watercolour. Cats are believed to have been introduced into Japan from China in early medieval times, with the first native Japanese kittens being born, according to tradition, in the imperial palace at Kyoto in the year 999AD. In sharp contrast to the often appalling treatment meted out to them in medieval Europe, cats were always well treated and as highly regarded in Japan as elsewhere in the Far East. They have also appeared in Japanese art for centuries, particularly in painting and sculpture.

◁ **Cat on a Windowsill, The Festival of the Cock, Asakusu Ricefields**
Ando Hiroshige (1797–1858)

Print

ANDO HIROSHIGE was one of the most popular graphic artists and print makers in Japan in the first half of the 19th century. He worked in Edo, the seat of the Shogunate which, after the return to power of the Emperor in 1868, became Tokyo. Among Hiroshige's many series of prints, one called *100 Views of Edo*, from which this print comes, is particularly attractive. The cat shown gazing out over the Asakusu ricefields is a Japanese Bobtail, an ancient breed. The cat has a very short tail, which looks even shorter because it is curved, the end hidden by long hairs which grow in a pom-pom. This is the cat which, drawn or sculpted with one paw raised in a gesture of greeting, has become a symbol of good luck, called *Maneki-Neko*, in Japan.

▷ **Interior of a School,
Cairo** c 1850
John Frederick Lewis
(1805–76)

Watercolour

EGYPT AND THE MIDDLE EAST
had long held a particular
fascination for British writers
and artists, partly for the
region's Biblical associations
and partly because it was
familiar to so many British
people as part of the overland
route to India. John Frederick
Lewis, a particularly fine
watercolour artist, lived in
Cairo for ten years from 1841,
producing in that time a wealth
of superb, finely detailed
watercolour studies of life in
Egypt. Since his observation of
the life of Cairo was so acute,
we do not question the fact
that the cat in this watercolour
looks just like an ordinary
family cat, with none of the
slender outline typical of the
cat of the ancient Egyptians, as
it may be seen today in such
cats as the Abyssinian and
Eygptian Mau.

◁ **The Reproof** c 1860
George Bernard O'Neil
(1828–1917)

Oil on canvas

AT FIRST GLANCE, it would seem
that both the girl and the cat
are being reproved here, the
cat for stealing (or eating) the
flowers in the vase on the table
and perhaps for trying to steal
eggs from the basket, and the
girl for letting the cat do so.
But the girl has a beribboned
bonnet hanging over her arm
and there is a young man
waiting at the door . . . Perhaps
the girl has been out without
permission, picking flowers by
the wayside when she should
have been busy about her
household tasks. Victorian
artists like the Dublin-born
O'Neil, a prolific painter of
genre scenes, produced gently
moral pictures like this by the
hundred, with cats often
introduced to give a quietly
domestic and feminine note
to the scenes.

△ **Best of Friends**
Henriette Ronner-Knip (1821–1909)

Oil on panel

HENRIETTE RONNER, born in
Amsterdam in 1821, seemed
destined from childhood to be
an artist, and had her first
exhibition at the age of 16. She
was one of the most successful
of the school of animal artists
which grew up in 19th century
Europe, selling her paintings
to an appreciative public in
many European cities.

Concentrating on cats, she
produced hundreds of
increasingly sentimental pictures
during her long career.
One well-known Victorian
biographer, M H Spielmann,
went so far as to call her cat
paintings 'masterpieces', a view
not shared by today's art critics,
who tend to dismiss her, a little
unfairly, as a nonentity.

▷ **A Bit of Cheese**
Henriette Ronner-Knip (1821–1909)

Oil on canvas

HENRIETTE RONNER-KNIP'S
fine observation of animals
extended to the settings in
which she placed them. One
of the attractions of her
best paintings today – and
technically, some of them are
very fine indeed – is the
glimpses they give us of life
in middle-class Victorian
houses. In this painting, the
antics of the family pets are
taking place in a dining-room
only recently left by whoever
had been enjoying a quiet
read of the *Scotsman*
accompanied by a glass of wine
and a bite of cheese.

▷ **Olympia** 1863
Edouard Manet (1832–83)

Oil on canvas

CATS HAD BEEN DEPICTED in art as a kindred spirit of courtesans and prostitutes for at least a century before Manet included a coal-black cat – in medieval times a familiar of witches – in this notorious painting, which caused a storm when it was exhibited at the Paris Salon in 1863. Manet intended his picture to be a modern version of Titian's *Venus of Urbino*, but where Titian had included a pretty little dog in his painting, Manet put a cat at the feet of his Olympia. In fact, Manet liked cats and put them in several paintings, including a portrait sketch of his wife in a pink peignoire with a black and white cat on her lap. His superb lithograph drawing, *Le Rendezvous des Chats*, depicting a black cat and a white cat meeting on a Paris rooftop, was one of the highlights of the first modern book to study the domestic cat, Champfleury's *Les Chats, histoires, moeurs, anecdotes*, published in 1868.

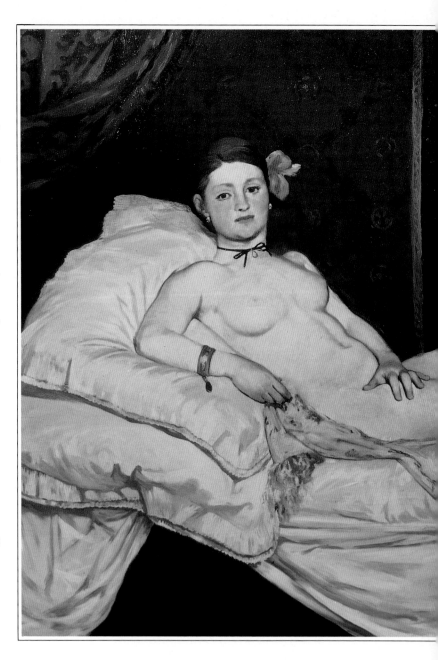

Detail

△ **Kittens at a Banquet** c 1870 Louis Eugène Lambert (1825–1900)

Oil on canvas

HERE THE CAT IS MOVING among the well-to-do in society – or, at least, among what is left when the privileged have moved on. The picture, painted by a very popular French artist much influenced by Sir Edwin Landseer, neatly sums up society's attitude to the cat at this time: pretty. charming creatures, but inconsequential, too, and certainly not to be considered as equal to a horse or dog, for instance. The cat and her kittens are perfectly ordinary domestic cats, – what we would call 'moggies' – for the cachet attached to pedigrees for cats had not yet acquired great importance among animal lovers. The holding of the first National Cat Show in London in 1871, followed by the formation of the National Cat Club in 1887, were signposts in the social revolution which saw the cat brought out of the kitchen and into the drawing-room.

△ **Reluctant Playmate** c 1870 Horatio Henry Couldery (b 1832)

Oil on canvas

HORATIO COULDERY was one of the most successful of the great number of competent 19th century English artists who found their niche, and made a respectable living, by painting sentimental pictures of animals, all too often marred by the artist's endowing the animals with human characteristics. The tabby kittens in this painting are beautifully observed, but giving the picture a title which turns both them and the mouse into versions of small children is not to today's taste. Even so, Couldery, who was a regular exhibitor at the Royal Academy between 1861 and 1892, produced many works which are increasingly sought-after; a painting by him of kittens at play, sold at auction in London for £300 in 1972, was re-sold for £4,500 in the mid-1980s.

◁ **A Modern Olympia** c 1873 Paul Cézanne (1838–1906)

Oil on canvas

WHEN CÉZANNE EXHIBITED this brilliantly coloured, exuberantly romantic picture in the first Impressionist Exhibition in Paris in 1874 one critic noted that 'M. Cézanne appears to be a kind of madman, stirred up while painting into a *delirium tremens*'. Partly in homage to Manet, Cézanne has chosen to paint the same subject as Manet's *Olympia*, which had also been harshly criticized when first exhibited. Like Manet, Cézanne has included a small pet animal in his painting. Unlike Manet, Cézanne would seem to have painted it too rapidly to be totally accurate – or maybe he did not share Manet's affection for cats. Judging by its long tail, we can guess that this is a cat, even though its head and ears are more suggestive of a small dog.

◁ **The Mousetrap** 1874
Angelo Martinetti (c 1850–80)

Oil on wood panel

IN THIS PICTURE, the artist, who
exhibited his work in London
galleries around the middle
of Victoria's reign, manages
to combine two lucrative
Victorian artistic genres –
animals and history – in one
picture. He also cleverly
forestalls any criticisms of
poor taste by putting the girl
lifting her skirts and showing
her ankles into an earlier age:
these are Georgian, not
Victorian young ladies. In
our own time, paintings like
this have become popular
as subjects for calendars and
jigsaw puzzles.

▷ **Girl with a Cat** 1875
Pierre Auguste Renoir
(1841–1919)

Oil on canvas

RENOIR, THE GREAT FRENCH
Impressionist, used the theme
of the girl, or young woman,
with a cat in several paintings.
This one is a relatively early
version of the subject, and
one of the artist's most
charming works, possessing the
delicately light and freely
handled colours of his best
work, but entirely free of the
sentimentality that could mar
the subject in lesser hands. It
has been said of Renoir that he
painted so many pictures of
girls and cats together because
he saw, in both, the same
qualities of sensual appeal and
charming playfulness.

◁ **An Interior with a Girl Playing with Cats** c 1880
Robert Collinson (b 1832)

Oil on canvas

HERE ROBERT COLLINSON, a genre painter who worked through much of the second half of the 19th century and whose *Summer Afternoon* was praised by no less a person than Ruskin when he saw it in the Royal Academy exhibition of 1875, seems to be harking back to the 17th century and the great age of Dutch interiors painting. As with the painting by Pieter de Hooch (see page 14), this one presents an attractively sunlit scene, with a range of rooms taking the viewer's eye into the

Detail

back of the picture. Now, however, the cats have been brought into the forefront of the subject, for they and the girl give the picture its sense of movement and action.

△ **Good Friends** 1881 Sir Lawrence Alma-Tadema (1836–1912)

Panel

LAWRENCE ALMA-TADEMA, the Dutch-born Member of the Royal Academy best-known for his prolific output of historical paintings, would seem to have fallen into the prevailing Victorian taste for sentimentality here. The climate of opinion which could lead Henriette Ronner-Knipp to produce paintings with names like *Best of Friends* and Sir Edwin Landseer to do an excellent study of two dogs, one large and one small, and call it *Dignity and Impudence,* has also influenced Alma-Tadema in the naming of his picture. Still, it is a very fine cat he has painted here, its attitude suggesting that the artist first observed it while it was stalking birds in the garden.

◁ **A Cat in the Window
of a Cottage** 1881
Ralph Hedley (1851–1913)

Oil on canvas

THERE ARE PROBABLY ROSES
round the door of this cottage,
for it is set firmly in the midst
of another of the strands
which made up Victorian art:
the romance of the country. As
there is nothing elegant or
stylish about the cottage, with
its everyday flowers in clay pots
and a ginger jar, so there is
nothing special about the cat:
just an ordinary, well-fed mog,
with his tail wrapped round his
paws in the neat way that cats
have. But Ralph Hedley is well
aware that most of us have
known cats like this, and
probably shared our homes
with a few of them, so we are
quite likely to be attracted
enough to his painting to buy it.

▷ **Julie Manet with Cat** 1887
Pierre-Auguste Renoir
(1841–1919)

Oil on canvas

THE GIRL IN THIS PICTURE has
been painted with such
wonderfully relaxed intimacy
because she was well known to
Renoir, being the daughter of
his very good friends Eugène
Manet (brother of Edouard
Manet) and his wife Berthe
Morisot, the Impressionist
painter. In the 18th century,
children and cats came to
be depicted together in art
increasingly often; by the
second half of the 19th century,
the convention had extended
to women, with no slur on
their characters intended. It
was not until the early 20th
century, however, that cats
came to be regarded as
perfectly proper companions
for men in portraits.

◁ **A Girl with a Cat** 1889
Théophile Alexandre Steinlen
(1859–1923)

Oil on canvas

A Franco-Swiss, Steinlen was
an artist and a cat-lover. He
kept so many stray cats in his
Paris home that locals called it
Cats' Corner. Many of his cats,
as well as those he observed
stalking the rooftops and alleys
of Montparnasse, achieved
fame as subjects for his posters
advertising such foods as milk,
chocolate and tea. His great
gift was to be able to catch
with uncanny accuracy a cat's
inimitable attitudes and
actions. In this picture, he
perfectly captures the actions
of the small child and the
reactions of the cat: we know
that the cat is going to tolerate
being humped about in that
undignified way and will
probably also endure having
the child's bonnet wrapped
round his head, because that
is the way that cats and small
children usually get on together.

▷ A Cat with a Fish in Its Mouth c 1890

Watercolour

THIS INDIAN KALIGHAT watercolour, of a kind painted by Bengali peasants and sold in the Calcutta bazaar to pilgrims visiting the Kalighat temple, was collected by Rudyard Kipling when he was in India. Indian paintings of this kind had some influence on the work of modern European painters, such as Fernand Léger. The cat on which the watercolour was based could have been a wild cat or a domestic cat, for India has known many kinds of cat, from the great tiger and Asiatic lion of northern India to the rusty-spotted cat of southern India and Sri Lanka. It is thought that the latter cat may be the ancestor of India's spotted cats today.

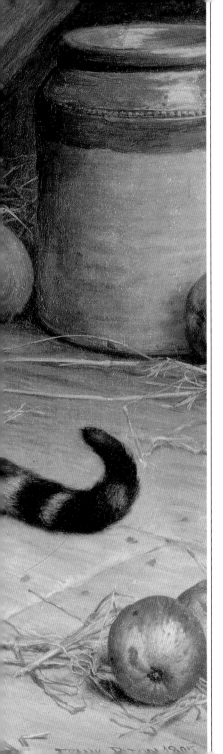

◁ **Alert** 1895 Frank Paton (1856–1909)

Oil on canvas

ANOTHER FINELY OBSERVED tabby cat stalks his prey in an attic, painted by a genre and animal painter who exhibited at the Royal Academy between 1878 and 1890. By the time this cat was painted British interest in cat breeding had become big business and the tabby, which had been the most common kind of short-haired cat in Europe for centuries, was having to vie for attention with such exotic foreigners as the Abyssinian, first brought into England in 1868, and the Siamese, the first example of which was given to the British Consul in Bangkok by the King of Siam in the early 1880s. Once called Cyprus cats, presumably because the cat's original appearance in Western Europe was via the Mediterranean trade routes, the tabby's name is probably derived from the fact that its markings are similar to those of a kind of watered silk made in Attibiya, a district in Baghdad.

▷ **Miss May Belfort** c 1895–6
Henri de Toulouse-Lautrec
(1864–1901)

Lithograph

MISS MAY BELFORT was an Irish
singer who achieved short-lived
fame – or notoriety – in Paris'
café-concerts' in the 1890s.
Toulouse-Lautrec first
encountered her at the
Café-concert Les Décadents in
1895 and did several paintings
and lithographs of her during
1895-6. He even designed
her Christmas card in 1896.
Toulouse-Lautrec usually
depicted Miss Belfort in the
Kate Greenaway-style dress
and bonnet and holding the
small black cat with a yellow
ribbon round its neck which
were the trappings of her act,
in which her most notorious
song, sung in a little-girl
innocent tone, began:

'Daddy wouldn't buy me a bow-wow, bow-wow,
Daddy wouldn't buy me a bow-bow . . .
I've got a little cat, and I'm very fond of that,
But I'd rather have a bow-wow-wow . . . '

▷ **Cats** 1899
William Henry Hamilton
Trood (1848–99)

Oil on canvas

BEST KNOWN FOR HIS STUDIES of
dogs, W H Trood also did
some fine studies of cats during
his successful career as an
animal painter. He also did
animal sculptures. Trood is
another Victorian animal
artist whose work has known
something of a renaissance in
recent years. Sotheby's, the
London auction house, sold
this painting for £3,520 in
the mid-1980s.

▷ **A Portrait of a Kitten** c 1900 Ada Eliza Tucker (c 1881–1928)

Oil on canvas

ESSENTIALLY a greetings-card artist, Ada Tucker had a worthwhile career that spanned nearly half a century, while her paintings, including this one, still have a good sale on greetings cards today. Her career coincided with the great boom in postcards at the turn of the century. The postcard was introduced into the British postal system in 1870 and soon become an enormously popular way of keeping in touch with family and friends. Cats became a postcard subject from the mid-1890s and in Edwardian times 'catland' postcards, as they were called by enthusiasts and collectors, outnumbered all other animals on postcards put together.

◁ **Hydrangeas** 1901 Philip Wilson Steer (1860–1942)

Oil on canvas

EARLY IN HIS CAREER Philip Wilson Steer, the son of a portrait painter, came under the influence of Monet and the French Impressionists, an influence strong enough to turn him into a leading British Impressionist. Although his painting from the turn of the century became more involved with interior subjects, in a strongly rococo style, he never lost the Impressionists' concern with light, as the wonderfully rendered sunlight and subtle play of light and shade in this painting demonstrates. Like other Impressionists, Steer also liked cats, both as pets and as subjects for painting. The black and white cat in this picture makes a perfect point of contrast with the light tones of the rest of the painting.

▷ **The Love Potion** 1903
Evelyn de Morgan
(1855–1919)

Oil on canvas

EVELYN DE MORGAN was one of several women artists working in the later phase of the Pre-Raphaelite movement. She had been a rebellious student at the Slade School in the 1870s and grew into something of a feminist as an artist, specializing in paintings of women full of an intense symbolism. She painted several pictures of witches, as if to prove that it was not a subject suitable only for the male artistic imagination. In this

Detail

one of a sorceress mixing a love potion, she has included a black cat, the witch's 'familiar' in folklore since medieval times.

Detail

◁ **Sleeping Beauty** John Dickson Batten (1860–1932)

Mixed media

JOHN DICKSON BATTEN was both an artist, having studied at the Slade School in London, and a barrister. As an artist, he was a painter, illustrator, a producer of colour prints and a fresco artist. He introduced into English art the Japanese method of cutting and printing from wood blocks. With this illustration of a scene from the fairy tale, *Sleeping Beauty*, Batten is introducing us to what has become in the 20th century a major home for cat art, the children's book. Sir John Tenniel could be said to have begun the tradition, with his marvellous drawings of the Cheshire Cat for Lewis Carroll's *Alice in Wonderland*; then there was Beatrix Potter, followed a generation later by Kathleen Hale with her books about Orlando the Marmalade Cat, followed in turn by many artists from all over the world.

◁ **Two Cats** 1910
Franz Marc (1880–1916)

Pastel sketch

THE GERMAN EXPRESSIONIST
painter Franz Marc, founder
with Kandinsky and others of
the Munich-based *Blaue Reiter*
(Blue Rider) group, found his
greatest inspiration in animals.
While his various versions of
the Blue Horse theme are
among his best-known works,
his vividly painted oil studies of
cats are also famous. This
beautifully observed sketch of
two cats was probably one of
many preliminary sketches for
the oil paintings, done in the
years before the First World
War, in which Marc simplified
the forms of the animals and
used pure colours not found in
the animals' natural condition
– red, yellow, blue – to create
abstract forms which would
express a total state of being.
Marc, who was killed in action
at Verdun, produced nearly 30
drawings, paintings and prints
of cats.

▷ **Afternoon at Home** 1922
Louis Wain (1860–1939)

Gouache on paper

DESPITE BEING THE SECOND
President of the British
National Cat Club, the artist
Louis Wain chose always to
draw the cat as a cartoon
figure, clothed and semi-human
– a caricature of the real,
naturally dignified animal.
Wain's popularity as a cat
artist, at its height at the turn
of the century, grew out of the
postcard craze of the day. He
had been producing illustrations
for books published by Raphael
Tuck, who also published
postcards, and from 1902
Wain's cat pictures began
appearing on postcards. Soon
he was 'Catland's' most famous
artist. When the postcard
craze died out, Wain returned
to book illustration, producing
many children's cat books
for the well-known publisher,
Dean, among others.
Towards the end of his life,
when the schizophrenia
which had long threatened
him became inescapable,
the cats he continued
to draw in great numbers
became extraordinary
creatures indeed.

◁ **Cat with a Basket** 1916
Charles van den Eycken
(1859–1923)

Oil on canvas

BELGIAN-BORN Charles van den
Eycken was one of many
European artists working in
the animal genre in the late
19th century. Competently
painted and beautifully
observed, charming and not
too sentimental, this cat
painting is an ideal subject
for birthday and greetings
cards. The artist has made
doubly sure of the success of
his painting by depicting a
Persian kitten, for Persians
were extremely popular at the
turn of the century. Even
Queen Victoria owned a pair
of blue Persians.

△ **The Cat** 1927 Tsugouharu (Leonard) Foujita (1886–1968)

ALTHOUGH THE JAPANESE-BORN artist Tsugouharu Foujita lived mostly in Paris, his devotion to cats, both in life and in art, was very much part of his ancestry, for the Japanese have been very well-disposed towards the cat for centuries.

Their cat art, as exemplified in the work of such 19th century artists as Kuniyoshi, has generally been mercifully free of the sentimentality which marred so much late-Victorian animal art. As this superb study of a tabby cat

demonstrates, this lack of a cloying sentimentality was a distinguishing feature of Foujita's work. As well as his many individual studies of cats, Foujita also produced a number of self-portraits with one or more of his cats.

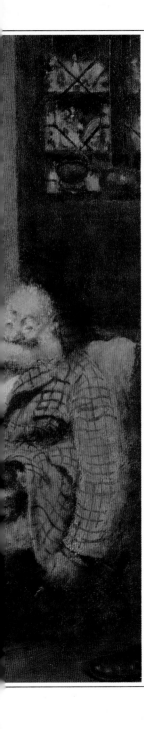

◁ **Sodales – Mr Steer and Mr Sickert** 1930
Henry Tonks (1862–1937)

Watercolour

HERE, THE MORE venerable end of the English between-the-wars art establishment dozes comfortably in front of the fire, probably after a good meal. Mr Philip Wilson Steer has a cat on his lap, also comfortably asleep, and Mr Walter Sickert has kicked off his slippers to reveal the full glory of his argyle-patterned socks. Henry Tonks, who paint-ed this delightful domestic interior, was a close friend of the two artists, having been associated with them in the New English Art Club. The year he painted this picture, Tonks retired as Slade Professor of Fine Art in the University of London, where he had taught many students who would later become famous artists.

△ **A Barn with Cat and Agricultural Machinery** c 1940
William Gaydon

Watercolour

WATERCOLOUR HAS LONG BEEN a favourite medium with British artists for recording aspects of everyday life. In the 1930s and 1940s, and especially during the Second World War, the British government actively encouraged artists to record all aspects of a society and way of life which showed too many signs of vanishing or changing irrevocably in the face of 'progress'. This fine watercolour, painted by a Cheltenham artist listed in a recent biographical dictionary of British artists as a wood engraver, is very much in that tradition.

△ **Cat with Everlasting Flowers** c 1987   Edward Bawden (1903–89)   Watercolour

EDWARD BAWDEN, who studied at the Royal College of Art, became one of that highly original generation of artists who gave British art so distinctive a style in the 1930s and 1940s. Book illustrations, prints, advertising art, even wallpaper design were all handled by Bawden with considerable style. He was an official war artist during the Second World War and survived being torpedoed in 1942. Later in life his preferred medium was watercolour and a favourite subject was his cat Emma Nelson, whose original name Nelson had to be made more feminine when the cat turned out to be female. The two came together in a delightful exhibition in London in 1987, the Private World of Edward Bawden, in which this watercolour was included.

▷ **Mr and Mrs Clark and Percy** 1970–71
David Hockney (b 1937)

Acrylic on canvas

ACCORDING TO HIS OWN account, David Hockney spent nearly a year painting this picture, a marvellously effective blending of traditional portraiture and modern, almost abstract style. One of a group of paintings of friends which forms a high point in Hockney's career, the picture has also become part of the iconography of the London of the 'Swinging Sixties'.

Hockney's friends here are the recently married Ossie Clark, a fashion designer and Celia Birtwell, a fabric designer, shown in their house in Notting Hill Gate in London. Incidentally, that's Blanche who has jumped on to Ossie Clark's lap; Hockney used the name of the Clarks' other white cat, Percy, in the title because he thought it sounded better.

◁ **Old Mr Tombs** c 1984 Ditz

Watercolour

'DITZ' IS THE PROFESSIONAL NAME of a present-day Austrian artist who has had considerable success painting cats, most of her sitters being either her own cats or cats of friends and relations. This picture, unusually for Ditz, includes many cats rather than the one or two she usually portrays. The inspiration for it came from George Orwell's story *A Clergyman's Daughter*, in which Mr Tombs, a retired bookseller, appeared. He 'lay in bed all day . . . with his long, dusty nose and pebble spectacles protruding from what appeared to be a fur rug of vast size and richness. But if you put your hand on the fur rug it disintegrated, burst and fled in all directions. It was composed entirely of cats . . .'

◁ **Cat on a Chair** 1986
Lucy Willis

Watercolour

LUCY WILLIS is a contemporary English artist whose work, charming and amusing without being sentimental, records the pleasant aspects of everyday life. Ladies in frothy hats at a wedding, a picnic tea set out on the lawn, the family's pet cat sitting on a kitchen chair: these are all subjects for her brush. To call her work greetings card art – and some of her paintings are indeed available as cards – is not to disparage it. Rather, it emphasizes the fact that where art in the 18th century found a popular market through prints, and in the 19th century through engravings, it now reaches a very large market through our continuing need, in a busy life with no time to write letters, to communicate with our friends.

ACKNOWLEDGEMENTS

The publisher would like to thank the following for their kind permission to reproduce the paintings in this book:

Bridgeman Art Library, London/National Gallery, London: *8, 9, 20, 21*; /**Prado, Madrid**: 10; /**Phillips, The International Fine Art Auctioneers**: 11; /**Galleria dell'Accademia, Florence**: 12-13; /**Harold Samuel Collection, Corporation of London**: 15; /**Wallace Collection, London**: 16; /**Louvre, Paris**: 18; /**Louvre, Paris/Giraudon**: 22, *26, 27*; /**Private Collection**: 19, 30, 31, 46, *47*, 69, 76-77; /**Private Collection/Giraudon**: 51; /**Roy Miles Gallery, 29 Bruton Street, London W1**: 23; /**Metropolitan Museum of Art, New York**: 24; /**Stapleton Collection**: 28-29; /**Victoria & Albert Museum, London**: 32-33, 53, 67; /**Wolverhampton Art Gallery**: 34; /**Bonhams, London**: 35, 41, 54, 58-59; /**Smith Art Gallery and Museum, Stirling**: 36-37; /**Musée d'Orsay, Paris/ Giraudon**: 38, *39*; /**Musée d'Orsay, Paris**: 42-43; /**Josef Mensing Gallery, Hamm-Rhynern**: 40; /**York City Art Gallery**: 44; /**National Gallery of Art, Washington DC**: 45; /**Hackley Art Gallery, Michigan**: 48-49; /**Laing Art Gallery, Newcastle-upon-Tyne**: 50; /**Petit Palais, Geneva**: 52; /**British Library, London**: 56; /**John Davies Fine Paintings, Stow-on-the-Wold, Glos.**: 57; /**Fitzwilliam Museum, University of Cambridge**: 60-61; /**The De Morgan Foundation, London**: *62*, 63; /**Christie's, London**: 64; /**Staatliche Graphische Sammlung, Munich**: 66; /**Gavin Graham Gallery, London**: 68 *(also used on front cover, back cover detail and half-title page detail)*; /**Tate Gallery, London**: 70-71; /**Cheltenham Art Gallery & Museums, Glos.**: 72; /**The Fine Art Society, London**: 73; /**Chris Beetles Ltd., London**: 78

Bridgeman Art Library, London/©David Hockney 1970-71: 74-75, 'Mr and Mrs Clark and Percy', 1970-71, acrylic on canvas,

NB: Numbers shown in italics indicate a picture detail.

Every effort has been made to trace the copyright holders and we apologise in advance for any unintentional omissions. We would be pleased to insert the appropriate acknowledgement in any subsequent edition of this publication.